THINKING ALOUD

Thinking Aloud

A Collection of Aphorisms

SIMON MAY

ALMA BOOKS

ALMA BOOKS LTD
London House
243–253 Lower Mortlake Road
Richmond
Surrey TW9 2LL
United Kingdom
www.almabooks.com

First published in Great Britain by Metro Publishing Ltd in 1999
Reprinted in paperback by Metro Publishing Ltd in 2005
This revised edition first published in Great Britain by Alma Books in 2009
Copyright © Simon May, 1999, 2009

Simon May asserts his moral right to be identified as the author of this work in
accordance with the Copyright, Designs and Patents Act 1988

Printed in Great Britain by TJ International, Padstow, Cornwall
Cover design: Øivind Ovland

ISBN: 978-1-84688-091-9

THINKING ALOUD

To find my home in one sentence, concise, as if hammered in metal. Not to enchant anybody. Not to earn a lasting name in posterity. An unnamed need for order, for rhythm, for form, which three word are opposed to chaos and nothingness.

Czesław Miłosz, *Unattainable Earth*

This delivering of knowledge in distinct and disjointed aphorisms doth leave the wit of man more free to turn and toss, and to make use of that which is so delivered to more several purposes and applications.

Francis Bacon, *Novum Organum*

CONTENTS

THINKING ALOUD

1

Relating

The better one knows someone, the harder it is to recognize them.

≈

It is less awkward to be humane than to be human.

≈

People who cannot stand solitude find it hard to be intimate.

≈

How marvellous to be seen; how perilous to be dreamt of.

≈

The highest joy of friendship – higher even than the delight of shared ideals – is to witness and defend another's life.

≈

Sometimes one can liberate others only if one is enslaved oneself.

≈

Tact is the most agreeable form of intimidation.

≈

Only the unreasonable expect others to be logical.

≈

Undesired praise can be as intrusive as unjust criticism.

≈

We often admire (or despise) people in order not to get to know them.

≈

To feel equal to others is almost always harder than to feel inferior or superior.

≈

Some enjoy others' suffering merely to enjoy their own safety.

≈

People(s) who are kindest to outsiders are often unkindest to each other.

≈

It can take more fortitude to sustain the tender emotions than the vehement ones.

≈

Vagueness can destroy human relations as thoroughly as can aggression.

≈

Jealousy imprisons – but is it not also a craving of the imprisoned?

≈

We are usually too slow to trust those we love and too quick to trust those we need.

≈

Almost everything can be tolerated – as long as we do not know what we want.

≈

Unshakeable patience with others can awaken them more powerfully than the best instruction.

≈

Judge a person less by his actions than by what they collectively make of him.

≈

The deep can be faster to fathom than the superficial.

≈

To seek "total love" is as illusive – and destructive – as to seek total knowledge.

≈

Greed often finds more pleasure in taking from others than in giving to itself.

≈

Guilt keeps one loyal to one's own values, shame to the values of people one needs.

≈

The only "natural enemies" are those who take one's very nature as an offence.

≈

Little is so strenuous as *keeping* someone soothed.

≈

Generous pity: to heed, embolden, defend another. Selfish pity: to hide, hijack, flee into, their distress.

≈

It is less suffering itself that evokes unbearable pity than *surrender* before suffering.

≈

Loneliness can be fiercest in the company of others.

≈

Insincere compliments should always be returned.

≈

Deep disputes get solved only after exhausting their relevance or their participants.

≈

We seldom convince anyone of what they do not already believe.

≈

Sometimes we trust only because prudence seems too arduous.

≈

Gifts from the generous unite; gifts from the mean divide. (The miser resents you for making his gift *necessary*.)

≈

Power over others can be the subtlest form of slavery.

≈

It is easy to be lawful, difficult to be just.

≈

Resilient institutions, like resilient marriages, transform goodwill from an occasional blessing into a permanent duty.

≈

Our hardest promises should be to ourselves; only by keeping *them* can we be true to others.

≈

Some admire their intimates only in order to admire their choices.

≈

Hear others' silence; heed their solitude. Otherwise they cannot be known.

≈

The terrible danger in the present age is to treat everything – and everyone – *experimentally*.

≈

A great friendship is always more exalted than either of its participants.

≈

Much can be tolerated only by forgiving it.

2

Timing

Nothing is deeply experienced – or revealed – unless one encounters it at the right pace. (Music, love, nature, knowledge…)

≈

The ambitious person has no time to hurry.

≈

Most ideas that appear "in a flash" have matured secretly for years.

≈

There is no greater danger to one's maturation than the headlong rush to define who one is.

≈

Reason's great enemy is not the cult of irrationalism – which still venerates the authentic – but the culture of speed.

≈

Life cannot be lived to the full by attempting to live every moment to the limit.

≈

All haste wears a death mask.

3

Gratitude

Sometimes only gratitude can bind us to what eludes our grasp – our past, our beloved, our world, our fate.

≈

Thanking, like thinking, must deeply engage with its objects if it is not politely to detach one from them.

≈

If we are to live life fully, we must not be *too* grateful to it – else we stifle the innocence and rebellion which, in due measure, a vigorous life demands.

≈

Gratitude can be our ultimate openness to the world; or it can be our last defence against misfortune – and perhaps the strongest.

4

Pride

The oldest consolation for failure: "He is successful, but I am purer, higher."

≈

Many accuse themselves in order to believe that they are better than they are.

≈

It is tempting to consider what is beyond our power to be beneath our dignity.

≈

For the hermetic pride, all intimacy is a trap.

≈

Narcissism, like vanity, is fossilized by self-*mistrust*.

≈

We tend to love our conviction more than our convictions.

≈

The charm of repentance is to ease the pain of errors – not to prevent their recurrence.

≈

The proud rely on their own self-esteem; the vain solicit it from others.

≈

Many who cannot save themselves long to save the world.

≈

Humility is commonly employed not only for making light of failure but also for refusing to be encumbered by success.

≈

Pride spins more lies than do even envy or ambition.

≈

Vanity is a hydra with many heads, lust a monster with only one – and by far the more tractable for that.

5

Loving…

We are all too often attracted to what is different in another, but nourish in them only what is similar to ourselves.

≈

The shortest distance between two lives cannot be a straight line.

≈

Love, in its extreme attentiveness, accumulates a great trail of doubts – and then, from its deep power of acceptance, *jettisons* them.

≈

To favour oneself over one's neighbour is easy; to love oneself over him can be a good deal harder.

≈

Intense self-content and -contempt can both drive one to love others – in order to flee the enigma of oneself.

≈

Lovers idealize not only the beloved, but themselves as well; for through love they visualize, however dimly, *their own* perfectibility.

≈

Open-ended receptivity to someone's reality can be more intimate than the most passionate devotion.

≈

The deeper a disagreement, the harder for both sides to agree what it is really about.

≈

It is a great mystery that another person can find in you a lifelong source of reassurance that you cannot for a moment detect in yourself.

≈

It can be easier, because more passive, to love those who hurt us than those who fortify us.

≈

To many who are hungry for love, poison tastes sweetest of all.

≈

Those who consider their love sacrificial invariably want it repaid in hard cash.

≈

To be the perfect spouse would ruin any marriage.

≈

In love some attack so as to surrender, others surrender so as to attack.

≈

To invite love is hard; to repel it is almost impossible.

≈

It is easy to be liked by people whom we do not love.

≈

Anyone who resents the intrusion and possessiveness of love resents the love itself.

≈

The mistrustful resist love for years, and then, exhausted by isolation, suddenly trust with arbitrary abandon.

≈

Dread lies near the beginning of love – of man as of God.

≈

Solitude is best when it can be shared with a loved one.

≈

Love makes much possible, but little attainable.

≈

Love's wisest demand: that the other person return to himself.

≈

Love's darkness: to live the other's deadness.

6

...And How to Stay Loved

No relationship would be sealed without mutual incomprehension.

≈

People *continue* to like us mainly for the weaknesses of our strengths.

≈

Tenderness, playfulness and reverence form the centre of gravity of all love – without which it lacks balance and fails to mature.

≈

Relationships are most deftly cemented by their sadnesses.

≈

The faults of loved ones can be tolerated and even enjoyed – provided they have nothing in common with one's own.

≈

To remain in people's affection it is safest to be dead.

7

Suffering

Many fuss over others' suffering – even God's – in order to forget their own.

≈

Some tolerate an inert life only by going insane on purpose.

≈

We excuse our mistakes in six ways: by diminishing them; by regretting them; by seeing them as inevitable; by focusing on their causes; by seeking the good in them; and by enjoying our survival of them. Here even the nonchalant are diligent!

≈

It is dangerously tempting to love life in general in order to escape life in particular.

≈

A little suffering creates a cynic; some more a pessimist; yet more a stoic; and enough an optimist.

≈

The destitute lack the safety to feel self-pity.

≈

Sometimes we forgive out of love, but too often we forgive out of *fear* – in order to imagine mastering an offender whom we feel too weak to avenge.

≈

Ingratitude is how we tolerate the burden of others' kindness.

≈

All suffering strives to establish its value – and so to "redeem" itself.

8

Deceiving

It is hard to succeed in the world without the skill to claim credit where it is not due.

≈

Fraud and deception are most strictly forbidden to those who cannot conceal them.

≈

Clever thieves do not steal; they lay claim – artfully.

≈

The proliferation of "rights" has greatly enriched the discipline of theft.

≈

Indignation enables us to lie with a good conscience – and, when merited, loses much of its charm.

≈

The eyes, far from being a window to the soul, can dissemble greatly; the mouth less so; the hands least of all.

≈

Sentimentality mimics passions that it wishes to enjoy but cannot experience.

≈

There are only two things which, given sufficient desire, close friends feel entirely justified in stealing: your books and your spouse.

≈

An act of weakness is most endearingly presented as a decision of principle.

≈

Our large faults are best concealed by parading our small ones.

≈

People always seem most naked when they are flimsily concealed.

≈

Affectations can be delightful embellishments – to a natural personality.

≈

Sincerity is the easiest virtue to fake.

9

Talking

People are more alike in speech than in silence.

$$\approx$$

Chatter about "creativity" paralyses creation.

$$\approx$$

Silence is the most insidious form of revenge – for *both* sides.

$$\approx$$

Solemn crowds are beautiful; solemn individuals are ugly.

$$\approx$$

Excessive talk silences the individual in one.

$$\approx$$

A real listener hears you even when you keep quiet.

10

Knowing

What cannot be taught always needs the greatest learning.

$$\approx$$

To know much is easy; to digest much is hard.

$$\approx$$

Every discovery is also a recovery.

$$\approx$$

Only a light spirit can bear heavy knowledge. (More generally: how the light supports the heavy.)

$$\approx$$

It can be easiest to tell the truth when one is not being sincere.

$$\approx$$

To the extent that thought is an ordered relationship between *experienced* passions, thinking and feeling are one.

≈

To find oneself stretched between opposed convictions can be the spark of life – and, in a well-formed character, the sharper their contradictions, the brighter the light.

≈

To succeed, one must question the value of one's works, but never the value of one's work.

≈

We can deeply love what we do not know, but we cannot deeply know what we do not love.

≈

We find the universal only after prolonged encounter with the particular – and only if we do not grope after it too insistently.

≈

Good explanations end up turning the familiar into the mysterious.

≈

Irony is a marvellous spice of life, but a paralysing way of life.

≈

The homeless best divine the minds of others – including God.

≈

Experience no more makes us wise than hearing notes makes us musical – for both demand the prior capacity to discern *innate structure*.

≈

One *really* knows only what one's nature and experience prepare one to know. All other knowledge is for distraction or titillation or prestige, and is consequently never understood.

≈

The urge to create – deeds, books, monuments, power – is inextricably bound up with the need to forget: that is, to so order the world that it will have no room for what we wish not to remember.

≈

The spirit – even more than the body – develops strength and subtlety only in small, indistinguishable steps. All great "leaps" just manifest an accumulation of such steps – or else are not genuine.

≈

Joy and pain not only go together, they grow together: for the commitments in which we find meaning usually bring us sadness too.

≈

It can take a lot of dung to produce an exquisite flower.

≈

The three transfiguring passions: love, despair and disgust.

≈

Doubt can attack one dogma only in the name of another.

≈

A mind that moves too swiftly cannot pause to think.

≈

Learning should always enrich one's ignorance.

≈

All maturation involves hard-won losses.

≈

Only a rich imagination can deeply fathom reality.

≈

One can grasp the world too powerfully to create it.

≈

Most acute presence of mind is also bodily.

11

Indulgence and Reticence

The best seducers are themselves the hardest to seduce.

≈

The great ascetic abstains not from sensuality but from love: indeed, only through sensuality can he tolerate this much larger denial.

≈

A reserve of crudity remains in even the most cultivated people, and without it the raw power on which refinement constantly draws would quickly ebb away.

≈

Everything beautiful feels at once intimate, unreachable and fated – and that is how it casts its spell.

≈

In all except the prodigiously gifted, intense experience demands sporadic asceticism: for the world *floods* in only if it is intermittently dammed out.

≈

Reason leads us away from our emotions – and then deeper back into them.

≈

Every life of extreme dedication is experienced as essentially artificial; yet only under unnatural pressure can a person's real nature flourish.

≈

To relish the extremes of discipline and dissipation, stability and chaos, implies no contradiction: for warring opposites relieve not merely each other but also one's inner deadness and disorientation.

≈

All fervency – whether for one's loves, one's hatreds, one's work, one's country – has the quality of prayer.

≈

Force seldom instils, or defeats, a belief – without the help of isolation.

≈

The morbidity of individuals is as unique as their smell.

≈

Every mood, including sadness, has its own coquetry.

≈

Passions mature best in a fastidious heart.

≈

Most people would be ashamed if they had never sinned.

12

Escaping

We all too often seek new opportunities so as not to seize existing ones.

≈

To take refuge in something – art, virtue, friendship, nature, God – unfailingly delights us, but is never the best way of knowing or honouring it.

≈

Modesty shields us from others, humility from ourselves.

≈

It usually takes several generations before a family can laugh at itself.

≈

When life gets too tedious, disgust quickly re-enchants it.

≈

The whole point of a good intention can be to avoid a good action.

≈

Many fight for their principles; few live for them.

≈

Truth likes to hide itself by stepping forwards as a formula.

≈

An eye (or age) too eager for paradox can blind itself to genuine contradiction.

≈

A great peril of feeling powerless is to seek a life immune to powerlessness – and so to the world itself.

≈

Few *émigrés* can halt the act of escaping – which only becomes more subtle, more arbitrary, more inward.

≈

The ability to forget and the inability to recall are altogether different skills.

≈

To live in perpetual hope can be a form of resignation.

≈

Absorbing, but not passionate, activity is the most durable of all sedatives.

≈

We can become so sensitive to pain that we no longer notice it through a haze of minor irritations.

≈

It can be all too tempting to abandon the risks of love for the pleasures of sympathy.

≈

The pathos of regret can blind us to our real mistakes.

≈

The only advantage of habitual pessimism is to protect one from genuine despair.

≈

Earnestness of mood is a sly way of escaping seriousness of purpose.

≈

To hide inconspicuously, choose the company of aliens.

≈

Sometimes privacy can be secured only by forcing others to despise one.

≈

One can become a parent without training – but not a butcher.

≈

Most criticize the world not to change it but to flee it.

≈

The stubborn are the hardest to pin down.

≈

Indecisiveness is among the most principled of all passions.

≈

The true cynic expects nothing more from life than confirmation of his disappointments.

≈

When disillusionment needs relief, it often turns romantic.

≈

The most powerful fantasies are those with the firmest roots in reality.

13

The Divine

It is indecent to invoke God merely to explain the incomprehensible.

≈

Among those harmed by idolatry we seldom count the idols themselves.

≈

Virtually any value, ideal or god can be employed for evil as well as for good; that it has been so employed is never, therefore, an adequate reason for abandoning it.

≈

Modern scepticism has left our religious hunger to scavenge for scraps of superstition.

≈

To save gods from being desecrated by men and men from never regaining trust in gods, it is in the interests of both men and gods finally to keep a respectful distance from one another.

≈

The transcendent – a great presence that language cannot express and we cannot possess – may hide or be unheard, but will never "die".

≈

Culture, unlike civilization, is innately pious – and so are all its rebels and ironists.

≈

How unbearably lonely is the god who is only either worshipped or denied – and who cannot end this isolation even by becoming man.

≈

Science and religion fight – and unite – as only brothers can.

≈

All attempts to justify the possibility of evil – as, say, necessary to freedom or to attaining the good – are not only unintelligible but sacrilegious – for they presume to explain the ways of God from the perspective of a god.

≈

God – the timeless, monotheistic God – temporarily abolished ancestor-worship, but with his untimely "death" we *are* our past again, and without due deference to it we commit suicide.

≈

Only the pure are purified by religion.

≈

Who wants a god that is satisfied with humanity?

14

Finding Our Way

The most seductive goals enable us to find a path but to lose our way.

≈

New intentions and "fresh starts" are life's hardest narcotics.

≈

Our unrequited love has children too; we call them "our ambitions".

≈

Well-being, unlike passing pleasures, cannot be directly grasped, but a life of sustained devotion to things we love can sporadically bestow it upon us.

≈

To understand what we are, we may first need to understand what we are not – and sometimes this means temporarily entertaining, and even *becoming*, precisely what is most dangerously alien to ourselves.

≈

One's deepest values – those that years of doubt and opposition fail to undermine, but, on the contrary, strengthen – can only be discovered, never created.

≈

All joy – even in hitherto unknown territories – is a sort of homecoming.

≈

We cannot find ourselves unless we find good in the world.

≈

Few paths to health do not take a detour through sickness.

≈

We sterilize life by reviewing it before it has occurred.

≈

Better to have great love for little things than little love for great things.

≈

To be strong you must trust yourself; to be merely resilient you need not.

≈

Suffering may be life's great teacher, but few learn more from it than sufferance.

≈

Nothing really functions as a means unless we engage in it as an end.

≈

We necessarily believe more than we can know.

≈

To thrive one must be patient enough to build one's skills from the bottom up and incautious enough to throw oneself open to the four winds of chance.

≈

Seek yourself too directly – and you will discover nothing.

≈

"Conscience" is that alertness to guiding values – and to the need for guiding values – without which our finest powers are incapacitated.

≈

One can command oneself only if one can dedicate oneself.

≈

Without deadly opponents it is hard to find the *real* courage of one's convictions.

≈

We can believe in so much and yet take a stand on so little.

≈

Some freedoms can be conferred; most are attained by fighting the countless seductions of slavery.

≈

On the whole, we repudiate vices not because we find them wicked but because we find them vulgar.

≈

To create a persona mix four parts fakery with one part sincerity and stir well.

≈

Most virtues, untamed, can become as tyrannical as any vice – but because they fight for what we consider good it is much harder to detect their trail of destruction.

≈

Few discover themselves without pretence.

≈

We see because we have found a path; we do not find a path because we can see.

≈

Occasionally we can seek – and find – freedom only by building prisons for ourselves.

≈

The authentic is where home and exile meet.

≈

The superstitious usually get unlucky.

≈

So tenaciously do we cling to our inherited values that we can embrace new ones only in the name of the old – and any revolution in values or repudiation of one's age is, therefore, always incomplete.

15

Surviving

Many things are most lovable when we have *conquered* bitter disappointment in them.

≈

One does not get "beyond" anything unless one has been immersed in it.

≈

Few of our deep problems can be resolved; most must be outgrown.

≈

Suffering indeed strengthens – the strong.

≈

Most explanations bore us – except as consolations.

≈

We learn the real lessons of our blunders best when we are poised to repeat them.

≈

Misfortune cannot be mastered simply by practising detachment or justifying its value; one must first absorb its cold necessity.

≈

One must know what to look for if one is to know what to overlook.

≈

Most of the wounds inflicted by truth can be healed only by more truth.

≈

We always inherit the sins of our forefathers, but occasionally we are also able to repudiate them.

≈

The innocently punished fervently seek their crimes; the justly punished tend to be rather less diligent.

≈

There are four possible reactions to the horrors of the world – and so to the world itself: to justify, to ignore, to accept or to repudiate. (Of which the most popular – and nonsensical – is the first.)

≈

Frivolity is most resolute in those whom love has first exhausted and then eluded.

≈

The fastest antidote to a fear is *another* fear.

≈

Our feelings must remain vibrant, fresh, light – even when they are sad, even when they age.

≈

The past – like unrequited love – is always buried alive.

≈

Apology as anaesthesia.

≈

Some mistakes are too good to be regretted.

≈

Even more destructive than bad luck is our resentment of it.

≈

Few of our trials actually happen.

16

Ageing

It can take half a lifetime for one's different personalities to *trust* each other.

≈

Faces that age without maturing grow formless: dead before they die.

≈

It is an endlessly subtle and violent task to let go of infantility.

≈

People quietly disdain anyone they are confident of outliving, whatever his merits – for in this respect, at least, they are the victor and he the already vanquished.

≈

Wisdom and generosity often bloom in youth, but ignorance and magnanimity ripen only with time.

≈

A turning point in life is the realization that the opportunity for "fresh starts" is over. One then either harnesses oneself brutally, or fumbles for ever.

≈

It is sterile to contemplate the nature of Death, but empowering to think towards one's *own* death.

≈

The art of dying well should be at least on a par with the science of obstetrics.

≈

Youth has strength without patience, age patience without strength – but our best years have both.

≈

To see pure goodness in little children is an immaculate deception.

≈

The craving for health easily becomes a sickness.

17

Slandering

The laziest way to respect oneself is to resent others.

≈

We often condemn what we lack the nerve to confront – including ourselves.

≈

The lure of slander is the lure of all extremes: to believe in something with promiscuous clarity.

≈

A personality is most simply constructed on a scaffolding of hate.

≈

The urge to define oneself through revulsion for others – individuals, classes, races, nations – and the drawing of *genuine* strength from this enmity, is perhaps the most terrible fact of human nature.

≈

Hatred, like love, has a taste for its own sacredness – and thence for the sacred itself.

≈

Racism's overwhelming subtlety, scale and resilience are systematically underrated – especially by its victims.

≈

Hostility to something easily blinds one to its real faults.

≈

Malicious gossip is most distressing when it is true.

≈

Who doesn't cling to his scapegoats for dear life?

≈

Few forgive those whom they have wronged.

≈

Mischievous tales need the best wags.

18

Evil

Evil's six most subversive habits: to turn virtue over to the service of vice; to invert values in such a way as to make what is dead seem alive and what is alive seem dead; to shame another into repudiating what he naturally loves; to invoke the sacred to justify the corrupt; to incite jealousy, fear or hatred between people; to parade power-lust as *love*.

≈

Our greatest illusion about evil is that it knows it is evil; whereas, in fact, the most dreadful destroyers, and the ones most indifferent to forgiveness, are precisely those who "know not what they do".

≈

Though blood-lust can be aroused in almost anyone, more violence is fuelled by yearning for comfort than by joy in cruelty.

≈

Evil may be outwardly "banal", but inwardly it always rages – with confusion, despair, anger, pride.

≈

Brutality often invigorates itself by turning sentimental.

≈

Can extreme sensitivity to pain be a cause of savagery – especially in its more sophisticated forms – as well as a result? (The twentieth century.)

≈

Our cruelty has many means, including kindness.

≈

Hell is far more respectful than inhumanity: at least it grants its victims trial by a loving and omniscient judge.

19

Opening up to Life…

The distinction: disgust versus love – closure to the essence of things or openness to it. (And yet, *the* identity: for the one cannot exist without the other.)

≈

Many things refuse us intimacy unless we can already say farewell to them – and foremost among these is life itself.

≈

All ways home are a detour.

≈

To be contemporary one cannot be a child only of one's time; one should also seek adoption by at least one other century.

≈

Chance, like a lover, is one of those awkward things of which we must be simultaneously slave and master.

≈

Tentatively to praise what we find alien or distasteful can be the only way of approaching it closely, and so of properly determining our attitude to it.

≈

One gets to know the world best neither by immersing oneself in the fray nor by withdrawal into slowness, but by alternating between the two.

≈

All freedom is bought at the price of accepting constraint, dependence and inevitability – the constraint of self-discipline, the dependence of love and the inevitability of the world as it is.

≈

Relations between trust and fear are always immoderate: a little trust can banish a huge amount of fear, while a breath of mistrust can reap a whirlwind of fear.

≈

No one can inspire greater fortitude than the dead whom one loves – not even one's deadliest enemy.

≈

Before worrying about the future we should strive for precise attunement to the present – and only then might we divine what is to come.

≈

Our experiences must master us before we can master them.

≈

Hypocrisy is often the first step towards an open mind.

≈

Failure is life's magnifying glass.

≈

Solitude is good; isolation is bad.

≈

111

Humility as total listening; faith as total hearing.

≈

One can expand one's horizons only by imposing borders on one's spirit.

≈

Why are "live" and "love" separated by a vowel?

≈

To possess wholly we must submit wholly.

≈

Affirming engages; justifying estranges.

≈

Opportunities are best created by seizing them.

20

...And Closing up

We often evaluate things in order not to experience them.

≈

Gloom – like hope – can be our cosiest bolt hole.

≈

To want something too urgently is always to lose its essence.

≈

To deem all existence vain is itself a judgement of the utmost vanity.

≈

Meanness asphyxiates; generosity frees – oneself before all others.

≈

The famous usually become deaf to everything except applause.

≈

Sloth can be a full-time job – for those in a state of siege against life.

≈

Pragmatism is seldom a guarantee of realism.

≈

We often chase the "why" in order to blind ourselves to the "what".

≈

Truth is cruellest when it kills our love for something.

≈

Life is too easily spent somewhere between the exhaustion of negating it and the terror of living it.

≈

Those who want to be wholly right never seem to be wholly real.

≈

The final indictment by this age of critics will be that there is nothing left worth criticizing.

≈

Technology's most pervasive danger is not its power to destroy but its ingenuity to distract.

≈

Action is seldom as reasonable as inertia.

≈

Our age is intensely animated yet curiously detached.

≈

Can anything, even a thought, be *possessed* for long without evicting its magic?

21

Attaining Stupidity

Superlatives maim.

≈

Indifference lames the heart.

≈

Stupidity needs stubbornness to make it truly stupid.

≈

The inveterate spectator of life imagines that by chaining himself to the world with judgements he will finally become one with it.

≈

There is no surer route to a petty mind than an obsession with refuting the pettiness of others.

≈

Those who strain for great "vision" usually see only mirages.

≈

Whatever detaches makes stupid: above all, pride, mistrust and fear.

≈

What we measure we diminish.

≈

Many seek freedom in violently discarding their talents and judgement – while conserving a secret ballast of sanity to save them from destruction.

≈

Self-haters seldom see themselves clearly enough to be self-critical.

≈

Stupidity is mentor to whole classes of shrewdness.

≈

Our deepest beliefs are often our most superficial.

≈

Some large ideas find space only in an empty mind.

≈

Almost every "nothing but" that reduces the complex to the simple is mere hocus-pocus – which makes vanish what it seeks to explain.

≈

Dogmatism is vulgar, even when it is insincere.

≈

The wise are much more susceptible to fools than fools are to the wise.

≈

The yearning for truth, being a form of love, can foster terrible illusion.

≈

Most "realism" impoverishes reality.

≈

Complaining stupefies.

≈

Only greed will serve *any* god.

22

Meaning in Life

We can happily bear meanings that avoid life, but never lives that avoid meaning.

≈

Our world would be empty without our unrequited love for it.

≈

One's supreme values always seem absolute – even when one repudiates the absolute.

≈

To see meaning in one's life is to express exactly what one has become – and so is never a "decision".

≈

We value our choices more than we choose our values.

≈

The "fundamentalist" urge to rank the original above what developed out of it is no more reasonable than to deem the acorn superior to the oak.

≈

Great ideas are seldom refuted, just superseded.

≈

People – and ages – can practise abolishing a faith, just as they can practise believing in one.

≈

Our history, true or imagined, teaches us who we are – not how to act.

≈

It is rare to fathom what anything means to us except by experiencing its loss.

≈

Man *loves* the ethical only as his ultimate guarantor of order.

≈

The mere existence of something overwhelms all its other significances.

≈

One knows the worth of a value only by pursuing its consequences to their limit.

≈

Most pessimists do not despise; they are indifferent: they damn not with low value but with no value.

≈

The "digressions" of life often render an intensity of meaning that its overall trajectory refuses to yield.

≈

Few values can be destroyed by war. Fewer can ultimately survive thought.

≈

Three marks of all excellence: power, structure and refinement.

≈

One seeks meaning in order to find happiness (despite its attendant sorrow), but one does not necessarily seek happiness in order to find meaning.

≈

In a godless world, it all of a sudden takes courage to despise life.

≈

Modernity's self-torture: to repudiate itself in the name of *its own* supreme value – that of individual authenticity.

≈

Fanfares for "cultural diversity" have come just when most of it has gone.

≈

The world is increasingly greedy for its liberation and increasingly numbed by its liberty.

≈

What marks out the West is not only its craving for ideals, but its urge to abandon them.

≈

Only unattainable ideals can endure: for only they offer inexhaustible hope – and only they escape the banality of success.

≈

Must a civilization be fixated by time to be respectful of truth?

≈

Obsession with the "meaning" and "value" of everything cripples our capacity for intimacy with anything.

≈

Death is the end of time that gives all time its weight.

≈

Only human nature does not abhor a vacuum.

≈

The value of existence can never be justified – only affirmed.

≈

In the beginning was the word – but before that came the deed.

≈

Where there is sun, there are usually shadows.

23

Character

The incorruptible can defiantly withstand great loss.

≈

Simplicity is the most complex attainment – because it demands the most perfect conquest of one's inner chaos.

≈

One's mind must be fathomed in solitude and one's character in community, but neither can be developed except by immersion in both.

≈

If we cannot outgrow our destructive passions we must outwit them – by forcibly and cunningly imagining their opposites.

≈

Bad taste is a harsher indictment than bad judgement – for taste manifests the whole individual, and so can be neither an "error" nor, in its essentials, reformed.

≈

Self-knowledge always reflects a fine spirit but seldom creates one.

≈

Virtue without humanity can be as monstrous as humanity without virtue.

≈

The passion for justice has all the other passions ranged against it.

≈

Suffering is fertile only when it both purifies and fortifies.

≈

Talent must be dwarfed by character – or it will not only fail, but attack its owner.

≈

Unless we constantly hone the skill of listening, the lies pile ever higher – and even the most sincere are unaware of them.

≈

Intellect is blind without emotion, and emotion is formless without intellect.

≈

Everyone is born into slavery; yet only the few seek freedom.

≈

A broad education civilizes less reliably than a narrow set of rules.

≈

Fear is spineless when it realizes that you intend to subdue it – and shameless at all other times.

≈

One easily forgets to cultivate the talents – of discipline, attention and love – needed to cultivate all talents.

≈

Character and taste are cousins – and without them learning is arid, choice impotent, and emotion mere gesture.

≈

Only the generous can receive – wholeheartedly.

≈

Passion, proportion and judgement: the girders of the soul.

≈

A "free" will can trust itself – and especially its safety.

≈

Character, like "spirituality", is not gregariousness; it is form.

24

Corruption

Power corrupts, but powerlessness corrupts absolutely.

≈

Truth might not be absolute, but it can certainly be abused.

≈

To deify the human is to deaden it: everything in man is denatured by making it holy. (Art, love, virtue...)

≈

It is not ill-gotten gains themselves that presage disaster so much as the fatally liquid personality which pursues them.

≈

The ferocity it takes to resist inhumanity easily makes people inhuman – even if their nature is gentle... *precisely* if it is gentle.

≈

How many miscreants who are "only obeying rules" would *be* anybody without the rules and without the obeying?

≈

Envy fastens only on what it can imagine enjoying. The unreachable it merely admires.

≈

Always seek the noblest company – a hard rule where we crave companionship, for the ignoble have a sixth sense for that craving and are the first to fuel and feed it.

≈

Those who exaggerate everything lose conviction in anything – even themselves.

≈

A life dominated by fear and hope dissolves the character, but leaves our cruder appetites perfectly intact.

≈

The cruel are seldom so unhappy: for they deaden their own sensitivity, love and discernment, and thus the sources of most unhappiness.

≈

To isolate oneself from the world out of disgust at its corruption is dangerous – for isolation quickly makes one disoriented – and thus corrupt.

≈

The greatest danger of despair is to see the ethical as pointless.

≈

Captivity corrupts its captives – by forcing them to *love* it.

≈

A person's taste can never be eradicated, but can easily be incapacitated.

≈

Incessant judgers never dispense justice.

≈

The indifferent are the most uncritically critical.

≈

Not all impatience is a vice, but all vices might be forms of impatience.

25

Self-esteem

Self-esteem can be so arbitrary – and precarious – because it largely depends on which pieces in our great mosaic of virtues and vices we happen to be attending to.

≈

We can no more grasp our inner life than we can grasp our internal organs.

≈

A little reason vindicates one's beliefs; a lot unsettles them.

≈

One's life can only be lived forwards and described backwards, but whether it can be understood, let alone justified, in either direction is very doubtful.

≈

The real beauty of admitting to errors is to furnish proof of one's existence.

≈

Praise is best from our superiors – from those who relate more deeply to our attainments than we ourselves can.

≈

Ambitions rarely satisfy; they are usually overshadowed by others or exhausted by time.

≈

Fame makes snobs even of the modest: for only clinging to each other reassures the famous of the resilience, grandeur and *fatedness* of their status.

≈

Peace of mind depends on the unprovable and is destroyed by the unlikely.

≈

Much sadness is merely weariness – whether from action or inaction.

≈

We can know our powers, but not our power.

≈

Only self-love can never be fully requited.

26

Values and Their Vices

Just as most virtues can be perverted into vices, so most vices contain the seeds of virtues.

≈

Values are cannibalistic. The idea that they tolerate "pluralism" is ridiculous.

≈

One of the mistakes fostered by truthfulness is to stop believing in truth.

≈

Loyalty, pity, forgiveness, self-sacrifice: all can be most ardently reserved for those we dread but dare not hate, reject but dare not flee, fear but cannot master.

≈

Certain flaws take superior talent, just as certain talents take superior flaws. (Love, courage, curiosity... we possess their strengths only when captive to their weaknesses.)

≈

What is excellent is almost invariably costly, but what is costly is not necessarily excellent.

≈

Irony, modernity's perfected art, playfully poisons the very culture whose "absolutism" it set out to cure.

≈

To seek perfect autonomy is to treat everything – especially oneself – provisionally and thus unseriously.

≈

Novelty has become so automatic that it will soon need to be reinvented.

≈

For the sake of originality many prefer a desert where they can stand alone to fertile soils that others have already tilled.

≈

Nothing seems quite as old-fashioned as the latest fashion but one.

≈

Successful ideals never let you succeed.

≈

Raw power is cathartic, but vulgarizes. Thus it will ennoble only as a transition to something more refined.

≈

Indiscriminate tolerance confuses and coarsens our emotions – especially our childish emotions.

≈

We make necessities of our vices at least as often as we make virtues of our necessities.

≈

Moderation is undiscriminating: for it vindicates almost any practice.

≈

Do good and evil, however gauged, not only compete and coexist, but actually cooperate?

≈

All perfection is aggressive.

27

Freedom and Its Trials

Too many options can imprison us more imperceptibly, and thus more securely, than too few.

≈

In an age stripped of moral absolutes, conscience is, more than ever, our last court of appeal.

≈

It is with palpable relief that modernity has discovered "limits to knowledge".

≈

It can take far more courage, vision and discipline to sustain great happiness than to withstand long unhappiness.

≈

Joy, especially when prolonged, can be more unsettling than despair.

≈

The paradox of permissiveness: more individualism, less individuality.

≈

Small decisions seem "free", large ones fated – and even the proudest will enjoys this sensation of humility.

≈

The interpreter might "finish" the work of art, but the work of art allows few interpretations to finish *it*.

≈

Long-term prisoners seldom release their jailers.

≈

Freedom: found only if renounced, mastered only if negated.

≈

Most values that are open to justification are vulnerable to repudiation.

≈

Expressive fragments and well-honed effects may soon be all that stands between the modern spirit and chaos.

≈

Many can master a moment; few can master a transition.

≈

Everything comes to an end, but nothing is completed.